AF323160

Horse
Less
Press

POEMS

NATHAN HAUKE

Every
Living
One

Published by Horse Less Press in Grand Rapids, Michigan / horselesspress.org / Copyright © 2015 Nathan Hauke / All rights reserved / ISBN 978-0-9908139-1-0 / Cover art by David Ruhlman / Design and composition by Alban Fischer / Set in Avenir, Futura Heavy and Volkorn / Printed in the United States of America / First Edition

The Lord is a delicate hammerer

—R Johnson, *ARK*
("BEAM 30, The Garden")

Sewn

1/3

Turbulence sews   one into another

Grainy harmonic   lifts the opening of the loop

As melody

Pierces the metallic hiss of tape

To ring through a wound

Little leaf you remember

Shaking its branch   over the water

Origin and arrival   to see it and see it again

Angled loosely
into the ground below the swing set

Can't imagine how you feel

Years spent thinking/ not thinking about leaving
waste time in a garden. Hummingbird's
arterial jag between flowers sews my wrists
with blue thread. Green peppers squash blossoms
tomatoes near the shed two maybe three weeks from ripe
Road into the next place sweeter behind the tinny clinks of pop cans

          strung out together on fishing line

....

                    Cut

Deerfield

These are the sheer facts to salvage

Light bounces
off the surface   rings that collect in leaves
Aphids and Jesus bugs
Aphid   swells along the roof of the mouth   cuts a ribbon
Shadows and grass wind algae brown stones   *to sharpen, to bend towards*
the current's readiness—when the muck is stripped off   stones shine
in the dissonance of cicadas

A process of mapping
Learning the mirror and field guide, leaving them

A small bluegill elm leaves   rent blades of grass slide past—*a kindred impression*
but who can say *the order of things   and without*

Sections sliced out of an elm leaf

Mindful of the caterpillar's jaws

in ecstasy of light falling on ferns

Sewn

12 / 11 − 12

Fire near the husks of flowers *Sewn*

Traffic of miniature electric candy cane forest

Branches covered in webs compass the sun

Erratic twinkle light reindeer with its hind leg on the fritz nuzzles grass

See the others through a reflection of scattered leaves

Skeletal, perforated by twilight

Addicted to language

Horns catching the edge of the light like Christmas

~~Branches covered in webs   compass the sun~~

To my eyes a flower   etched in the glass of the front door

Busted pocket of ice near wet bark

~~Skeletal, perforated by twilight~~

Laying in wait   by an abandoned water dish

Mary Rowlandson: *I was alone*

And God was with me

12 / 11 — 12

At present

Crackle of static

Over the needle

A reindeer aches

To be located

Near lavender

. . . .

Water-swollen paint	*flakes off foundation*
Scratchy hemorrhage	*near the husks of flowers*
Where you've been	*a frozen river subject to thaw*
Rain dulls to opacity	*then sharpens towards clarity*
Reflects hall light	*doubled in the window*

Makes one for each eye before the optic nerve solders them together

What's behind me or whatever was

Lights up like a rifle shot

From the other side of the field

. . . .

Chatter stammering between two places

Current that dazzles behind trees   how many years ago

Wrote: *Salvation speeds towards the wreckage of salvation*

Deerfield

Crossed by branches

I am constrained to acknowledge large sections of paper
sag loosely around the birch's trunk—a chrysalis
covered in orange stretches of light

There is   must be *a higher origin of*

Rotten branches and wraps of skin litter the wood's floor   milky grey
with black flecks—clear   distinction from moss
burnt needles   withered leaves drifted in
from neighboring maples

Must have been a bridge—

Bushes grown out of stones on the cut bank
        Two splintered posts stand shoulder-height
near dry tufts of hay   and field grass. Here before the tumor swelled to
cause the seizures.
Left on *this* bank   a post   stands the same. Another on the right
is broken off at shin length.
Pine's slow sap   nests mute in absence of sparrows
paramedics   swarming into
the house. Needles forked through
elm branches   suspended. Only they couldn't get the tube because they couldn't
get him to stop shaking

Parson Hooper

Guilt was a light switch. Guilt was a stale crust of snow—a mousetrap

Guilt was a mirror—a page torn from a magazine

Guilt was moving and it kept moving—

Your soul looks like garbage scattered through bleachers—a staircase

broken off between floors. Your soul your secret sin—gunk and

change in the car's cup holder. Your soul is a weathered coil of blue hose

next to an empty pool at the Howard Johnson

I was eight ten twelve years old when I was saved—

Standing in the dark where cattails have broken through snow

I turned toward the lights of our house

from the rink we were clearing in soaked mittens—"God's mercy is greater

than God's wrath, but God's wrath is terrible." *Your hands*

your hair your true face—

Not yours.

The glazed sky coughs like a bottomless pit

Snow banks flicker and shred the glare of street lamps

into millions of tiny crystals—

Faith

Attends delicate hammering   breeds presence

Where there is no work

. . . .

What's beneath the surface

Simply the other side

> *Restless ebb of faces in pictures*

As resonance proves fertile

> *While a sweet dog puts his nose into your hand*

Grounds for music

Amber tracks of sky   twisted through branches

Cattails insistent across the way

Where ice glows in twilight bright red

Saccade of taillights past the bridge near the Plaza

You used to rent videos

You used to cemetery across the street

Graved in the bark of the maple

Blurred white

Birdhouse

Steady

Bloom

Rising through

Splintered distortion

. . . .

A thin shelf of ice   above water

Dingy garland adorns   railing at intervals

It's thirty degrees   near the sugar maple (heat)

Concentrate on a leaf shaking its branch

Loosen a little terror in my throat

     orange

spiles.   lighter where current goes wide

     Traces of black   pulpy leaves in
my throat
the telephone

     blood soaking into   carpet
A stale drift of snow   ice   scuffs

     hangs   out over

12/24—27

Sun abraids ice

To current

Sharpens an edge

Waiting

A satellite dish

In the yard

Sometimes just can't

See the activity

Only it's gone

Paw prints in snow

Fossil of playtime

"Radio Amor" :: spillage

The crackle of static   errant buzz of light

Over the wing sticky

Refracted through bottles of cheap wine

Water SKYY vodka

Oceanic loops of feedback

Turbulence to weather

Sketch

Loose black sheet plastic

Flapping beneath *Aspen* little white flowers   wasted in extravagance

Pink threads of cloud   crash in webbed bottleneck

The sweet smell of bread from the Wonderbread factory

Thoreau put his ear right up against the telegraph pole

1

winter scours my eyes with steel wool and they shine like coal

and they fill with wild apple blossoms jet-black feathers

and they grainy edge where dusk bleeds through brittle leaves a

rusted-out coffee can

2

Or last night

crying again

You really

wanted to be pregnant

even though

we can't

afford to

buy groceries

3

Intent on dry weeds—

Double-exposure   a face that ghosts itself in the photo

Stale ice flows scraping orange buoys

Trash wrappers torn up through trees across the field

after Mom calls to tell Noah they've taken Grandma to the hospital

when they can't get her out of the chair

4

IRIS

Names loved ones radio static   smoke

Ventilator sunlight twists

the oak's broken shadow

Voice ripped free to drift

or the crow's flight to his branch

5
For Kirsten

It's a fine morning

. . . .

He was bent over crying on the stairs

Stepping out onto the deck   to fish beers out of a snowy 12-pack

Wind rattles trees streaked by intervals of distance—Panicked hum

buried in the hem of each frame   A glossolalia of wings

where seed eats through   near the base of the feeder

6

Draft of wind

just over

the flue—

Ashes

As far as

what

grieves you

Ashes

It's gone

Forever

grieves you the most

7
Sassy

Carolina wren

laughing

its head off

Melt on the deck

near old leaves

and a bunched-up rug

8

Sweet rot

oranges

Musty

week-old bouquet

Snow covers the river

a knit throw

The morning

you died

woke us up

and we were

shocked

Dogs howling

9

F smacks his lips to lick out an empty yogurt container

Holes or wounds savage shaking in the air

as dead brothers wave at the window

Your soft hands   arms like bark

Looking up from somewhere frightened

Blistered heat of coals in the woodstove

Leave Noah sleeping   across two chairs by the bed

Your hair like cornhusk

10

Bent corner post

got some give to it

Deer crowd

worn tombstones   for winter grass

Simple and they return   gracefully

not cut off from each other   nettlesome

haunted by dissonances

11
House at THE LITTLE ANGELS OF HEAVEN in shadows vacant all day

No one's there since the man went to jail for assault

12

Make a home where you are

wrap K in our quilt and pull on my jacket in the doorway

Brush snow off the woodpile dirt and ash

from my hands at the sink

Mourning is slow music

bubbles under the ice

buds gathering behind isolations

residual numbness of grief—hoarfrost

on faded cloth flowers

13

Feedback—

Raw knot of gratitude

        racked by anger

Frayed blue tarp

        shuddering in a crosswind

Buckets of ash

        we pour into the garden

Leaves crushed to pulp

        under the chair's legs

Cloud Like

A plastic grocery bag   tacked to the top of a pine

Dusty window   slanted against a pile of bricks

Shredded VHS tape that glitters in the median

F's

Sick in the yard near the blue table

Walks the perimeter eating grass

Torn through our fence by the teeth

Corner of dirty light near the steps

Asking for a little magic

....

Hazard feather   adjacent the trunk

That was days ago already

12/29—1/2

~~Mary Rowlandson:~~ *I was alone*

~~And God was with me~~

Snow catching in pine branches colors

Sky green few dry leaves

In the window turn snow

Burnt orange scattered

Like color away from home

The rest is activity

My mother's birthday—

One edge rests another

Commotion of wet latticework

Melt more like a feeling

Ornamental garden ducks

Stranded in winter grass

Last summer's chairs

Lean against a glass patio table

Beads of condensation

Streak green grill hem

Meaning these traces

Won't come into focus

Deerfield

The *flower spike is 'not square'* each blade contains   *2-9 flowered spikelets*
below spikelets not stiff with   *slender keel and ribs*
Outside, grass is thicker light wet
fresh looking. How to express differences   light's persistence
mutable by foliage. Psalm 31: *Let your face*   *shine on your servant save me from*
your unfailing love

Uses for quack grass   include: *diuretic for 'gravel' (kidney stones)   worm expellent*
wash for   *swollen limbs*

Into New Affections and Noise

1

Magpies sew heat through branches *M-A-G-N-O-L-I-A* where light

Graves in mind an answer

2

Light's grave in mine

Hard to swallow

M-A-G-

N-O-

    L-I—A

There is this feather

Falls

Into my hands

While my hands rush up

To meet it

Deerfield

A sheet of ice   thick enough to hold tracks
. . . .

Location cuts sharpened to an edge against current
where I reach toward
the dry crack of branches as snow softens enough to cave in
layering the surface. Orange-brown leaves rake diagonals of wind
Laid beneath another river. Psalm 63: *I sing*

    in the shadow of your wings

Blue Rags
Stitched Together
by Crows

For Levi

Home moves to begin in hell or otherwise

Crows etch hieroglyph Xs

Across our eyes

Mark time

At the edge of accounting

Their husky *caw*

A black stitch

From one crown

Into another

Morning's work

Civility—

A gnawed-at Indian corncob hangs from a screw in the eaves

Wrenching the shanty nails loose with the teeth of a borrowed hammer

To spin the slats and bring them down   *Where there is no house*

And no housekeeper

Snowed-in in *IN*—

Snow christening the frames of reindeer

~~Pierces the metallic hiss of tape~~

Glass another surface   *painful to shine*

Between chatter and the recording

Mute as a crushed pie tin flashes   *through atmospheric gradations*

Where an angled length of roof   extends into the dissolve

Fur that drifts over the vase's concentration

Vision   a tangle of stalks that flowers

Josh's birthday today—

Cellophane wrappers for shortbread cookies

Stanley Cavell:

The conditions of meeting upon the word

Are that we

Know how to depart from them

Alive and well

Stray Music

For Kirsten

1

blossom in a wreck of nervous energy

one translation: no job and no money how we'll get through the summer
how we'll take F to the vet if his leg doesn't get better
shadows of leaves overhead settle on the door
through the screen like a trapped animal
exhausted

. . . .

light spilling through busted latticework   a set of antlers hanging from the roof

you're gone for the weekend but I wish you were here

talking like every morning

2

music startled up from grass

our crooked telephone pole trembling in a crowd of drunk robins
our little house swimming across the windows of the house out front

all this syrupy chatter   elongated slats from the neighbor's fence
stretching through ours
cracked white paint flakes what's in mind
depends on what happens   loose feathers in shreds of leaves by the steps
scratchy talk radio: health care reform   suspected terrorists
expected to be out of the country

. . . .

suffering something like green clover takes over the yard
happily worn down to dirt where F is sleeping

a few ants in ashes near the rug

3
like a plastic flower pinwheel

blasted in sun after a long absence

mocking bird you are a rusty porch rail
abrasive throttle of a monster truck
 juddering down the block while I lumber in the doorway
Saturday afternoon weeds across the steps

you move where the light goes

4

window in the floorboards   thirsty as yellow snapdragons

flat sheen of black chokeberries vent wind

pixelated red body of the truck parked behind

I remember thinking each verse of the hymn

was like a room in a house

book I set down   another angle along the grain of the table

the truck's mirror sparks through a river of leaves

F's taped-up paw in the sun   smell of spring air

a mirror to know we are apart

all this distance composing a field

holds

Acknowledgments

Thanks to dear friends and family for all of this company, especially Kirsten Jorgenson, Gus, and Frankie.

Thanks to a few folks, in particular, for sustained close readings of these poems and insight into their organizational structures at key moments: Kirsten Jorgenson, Brenda Sieczkowski (with her diamond-cutter's eye), Mike Sikkema, Jen Tynes, Shira Dentz, and G.C. Waldrep.

Thanks to Donald Revell, Joseph Lease, Donna de la Perrière, Hank Lazer, Craig Dworkin, Paisley Rekdal, Karen Brennan, Pepper Luboff, Ely Shipley, Gina Myers, Hazel McClure, Caroline Klocksiem, Geoff Babbitt, Kathryn Cowles, Cami Nelson, Eryn Green, Christine Marshall, Stacy Kidd, Derek Henderson, Jen Denrow, and Erika Howsare. All you working doggers. All the fossils left in the dirt.

Every living one sewn through every living one.

Thanks to David Ruhlman for the use of his gorgeous handmade book, *Felt* (2004), for the cover image.

Thank you to *Poets In Need* for help when we really needed it.

Thanks to the editors of the journals where these poems first appeared in various forms: *American Letters & Commentary; BlazeVox; Colorado Review; Denver Quarterly; Electronic Poetry Review; Eleven Eleven; EOAGH; Forklift, Ohio; Free Verse; Greatcoat; Horse Less Review; Interim; Parthenon West; Route 7 Review; Spittoon; Spork; Twenty Six; TYPO; Word For/ Word; XANTIPPE;* and *Zen Monster.*

Thanks to Jen Tynes, Jen Denrow, and Erika Howsare at Horse Less Press for publishing *S E W N* as a chapbook (2011). Thanks to Gina Myers and Lame House Press for producing a limited edition chapbook entitled *In the Living Room*, which included early takes of some of these poems (2010). Thanks to G.C. Waldrep and Joshua Corey for including "Deerfield" (1) in *The Arcadia Project: North American Postmodern Pastoral* (Ahsahta Press, 2012).

These poems often return to *Walden* and to the compost of Henry David Thoreau's *Journals.* "Sewn" riffs on Mary Rowlandson's *Of the Captivity and Restauration of Mrs. Mary Rowlsandson* and draws from Stanley Cavell's *The Senses of Walden.* The "Deerfield" series absorbs text from The Audubon Society Pocket Guide: *Familiar Trees of North America,* The Audubon Society's *Field Guide to Wildflowers: Eastern Region, and Paterson Field Guides: Eastern-Central Plants and Herbs,* Psalms, Ralph Waldo Emerson's "Nature," "The Over-Soul," and "The Poet." Parson Hooper is a character in Nathaniel Hawthorne's "The Minister's Black Veil." The title "Into New Affections and Noise" comes from Arthur Rimbaud's "Departure" (trans. Donald Revell).

Nathan Hauke

is the author of *In the Marble of Your Animal Eyes* (Publication Studio, 2013) and four chapbooks, most recently *Pastoral (years later)* (Shirt PocketPress, 2013), as well as a talk about getting a small press off the ground in a rural community, entitled *Country Music*, that was written in collaboration with his Ark Press co-editor Kirsten Jorgenson and published as a part of the DoubleCross Press *Poetics of the Handmade* series (2013).

He was born and raised in rural/ small-town Michigan and currently lives up on the ridge in North Carolina with his partner, Kirsten Jorgenson, their son, Gus, and beast, Franklin. He has a Ph.D. from the University of Utah. He is a poetry editor for *Coconut Magazine*.